BELL LYRA

HARVEY S. WHISTLER

A FUNDAMENTAL COURSE FOR INDIVIDUAL OR LIKE-INSTRUMENT CLASS INSTRUCTION

RUBANK®

HAL•LEONARD® CORPORATION

7777 W. BLUEMOUND RD. P.O. BOX 13819 MILWAUKEE, WI 53213

PLAYING POSITION

When playing the Bell Lyra, the mallet should be held in a firm and secure manner between the ball of the thumb and the first joint of the index and middle fingers. Using a relaxed position of the wrist, the player should produce the tone with a quick, elastic blow of the stick, being sure to strike each metal bar in its exact vibrating center. As it is obviously tedious to remain standing for any length of time, the player will find that satisfactory results can be obtained by practicing while in a seated position. The lyra itself may either be attached to the base of a concert stand, or placed on a smooth-surfaced flat table, low enough for its complete playing range to be well within full arm's length of the player. To prepare for parade routines, however, the player should, as soon as he has familiarized himself with the intricacies of the instrument, practice while walking to and fro, the Bell Lyra being held in playing position by means of the customary leather carrying strap and the left hand of the player.

TONAL SHADING

To produce tonal shading on the Bell Lyra there is no other alternative than to strike the bars of the instrument either lightly for soft playing (*p-pp*) or forcibly for loud playing (*f-ff*). Hence when practicing, the player should accustom himself to regulating the volumn of tone of the instrument through the amount of force directed into each blow of the mallet.

SPEED OF PLAYING

When one mallet is employed in the playing of the Bell Lyra, certain technical limitations with regard to speed impose themselves upon the performer. While it is perfectly possible to play 16th notes in $\frac{4}{4}$ measure on the Bell Lyra, they can be executed only at a moderate rate of speed, and especially is this true if they fall in skips of wide intervals. Furthermore, the continued vibrating tone of the lyra is of such a nature that there results a blurred effect when 16th notes or even 8th notes are played in rapid succession. If two mallets are employed in the playing of the Bell Lyra, the executant's scope of technical dexterity is increased manifold.

RELATION TO PIANO KEYBOARD AND RANGE OF BELL LYRA FAMILY

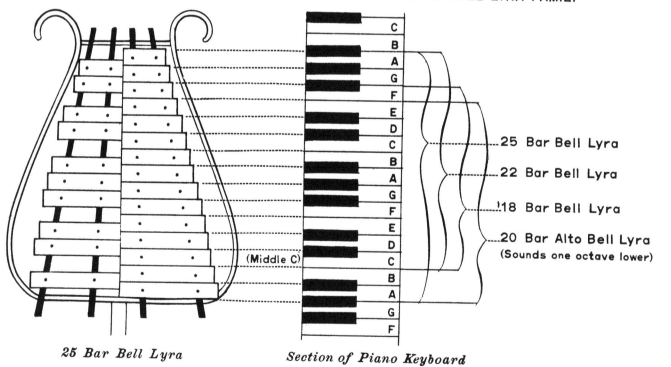

25 Bar Bell Lyra

22 Bar Bell Lyra

18 Bar Bell Lyra

20 Bar Alto Bell Lyra
(Sounds one octave lower)

25 Bar Bell Lyra   *Section of Piano Keyboard*

Beginning Bell Lyra

Scale of C Ascending

WHOLE NOTES

Produce each tone with a quick, elastic blow, striking the mallet in the center of the bar. Allow the pitch of each tone to vibrate freely for the full value of four counts.

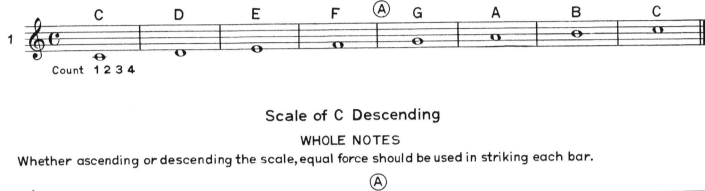

Scale of C Descending

WHOLE NOTES

Whether ascending or descending the scale, equal force should be used in striking each bar.

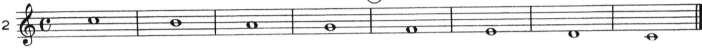

Scale of C Ascending and Descending

HALF NOTES

Be sure to hold the mallet in a natural and easy manner.

Extending the Range

Evening Song – Serenade
from "Paving the Way"

Copyright, MCMXL, by Rubank, Inc. Chicago, Ill.
International Copyright Secured

4

Introducing Quarter Notes

Etude in C

SCHROEDER

Jingle Bells

J. PIERPONT

Little Brown Jug

Traditional

5

Merrily We Roll Along

College Song

London Bridge

English Air

At Pierrot's Door

French Air

Yankee Doodle

American Air

Twinkle, Twinkle

MOZART

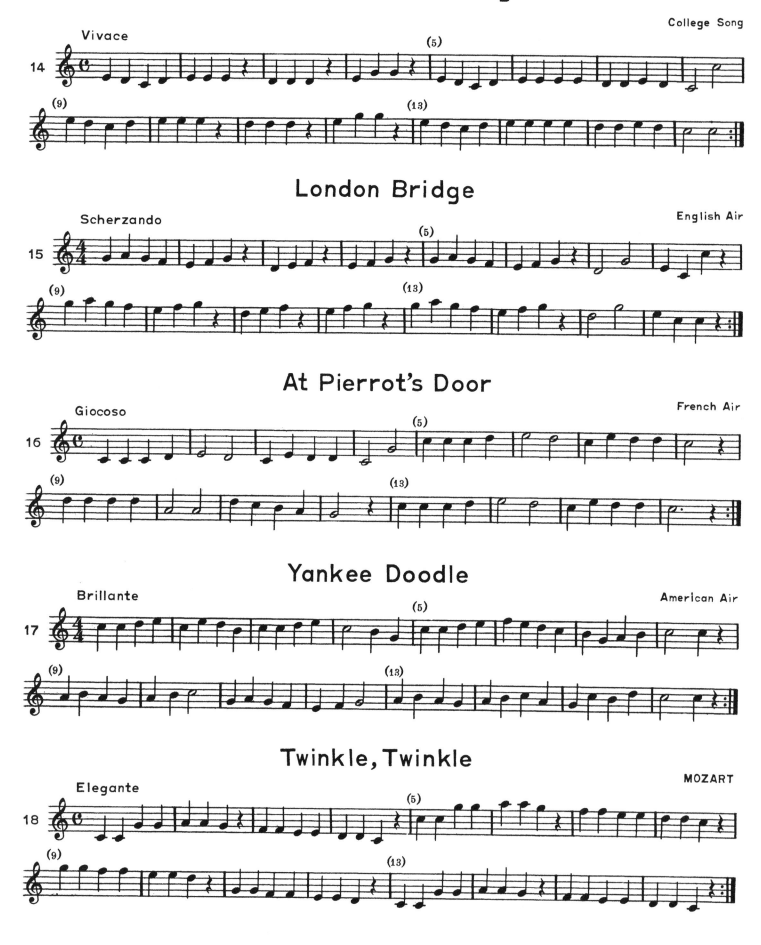

Old MacDonald

American Air

Mulberry Bush

English Air

Good King Wenceslas

Christmas Song

Merry Widow Waltz

LEHAR

The Chromatic Scale

Short Chromatic Studies

Interval Study

31

Octave Exercise

32

My Bonnie
Solo or Duet for Bell Lyras

Folk Song

First Bell Lyra (Melody part)

33 **Second Bell Lyra** (Harmony part)

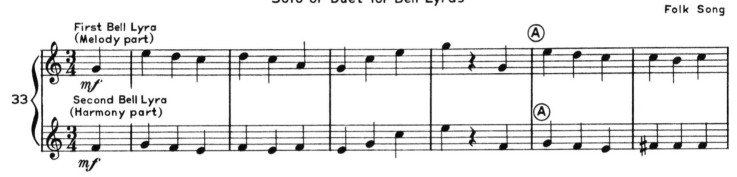

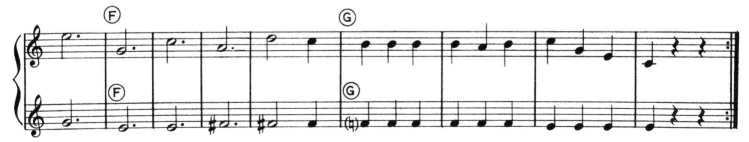

Introducing Eighth Notes

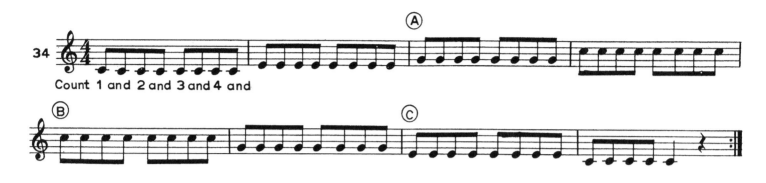

Count 1 and 2 and 3 and 4 and

Exercise in Eighth Notes

CUNIOT-HURY

Moderato

Quarter and Eighth Notes Alternated

Moderato

The Glorious Fourth

Old Colonial Melody

Con spirito

Introducing $\frac{2}{4}$ Meter

Soldiers Chorus
from "Fra Diavolo"

AUBER

I've Been Workin' on de Railroad

Solo or Duet for Bell Lyras

Pioneer Song

Introducing the Dotted Quarter Note Followed by an Eighth Note

By the River

WILLIAM BEACHLER

Oh! Dem Golden Slippers

JAMES A. BLAND

Anvil Chorus
from "Il Trovatore"

VERDI

All Through the Night

Old Welsh Air

America the Beautiful

SAMUEL A. WARD

Auld Lang Syne

Solo or Duet for Bell Lyras

Scotch Folk Song

14

Introducing Sixteenth Notes

Exercise in Sixteenth Notes

CUNIOT-HURY

Practice this exercise slowly at first

Quarter and Sixteenth Notes Alternated

Play strictly in time

Fierce Flames Are Raging
from "Il Trovatore"

VERDI

Agitato

Song of India

RIMSKY- KORSAKOW

Hunters' Chorus
from "Der Freischütz"
Solo or Duet for Bell Lyras

WEBER

The Key of F

Etude in F

SCHROEDER

Introducing $\frac{3}{8}$ Meter

The Campbells Are Coming

Scotch Air

Good Night Ladies

Introducing $\frac{6}{8}$ Meter

59 Count 1 2 3 4 5 6 1 2 3   4 5 6

Nocturne
Solo or Duet for Bell Lyras

VON BLON

First Bell Lyra (Melody part)

60

Second Bell Lyra (Harmony part)

18

The Key of G

Etude in G

SCHROEDER

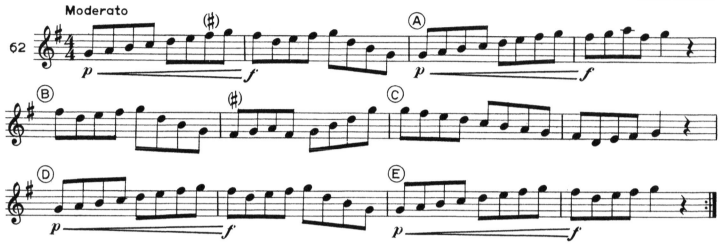

Tambourin

GOSSEC

Andantino

LEMARE

Amaryllis

H. GHYS

Home on the Range
Solo or Duet for Bell Lyras

American Folk Song

Just A Song at Twilight
Solo or Duet for Bell Lyras

MOLLOY

The Key of B♭

For 25 bar
Bell Lyra

Etude in B♭

SCHROEDER

Wedding March
from "Lohengrin"

WAGNER

Introducing the Dotted Eighth Note Followed by a Sixteenth Note

Air from Rigoletto

Solo or Duet for Bell Lyras

The Key of D

Etude in D

SCHROEDER

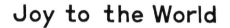

Joy to the World

HANDEL

Little Annie Rooney

MICHAEL NOLAN

Reuben and Rachel

Pioneer Song

She'll Be Comin' Round the Mountain

Solo or Duet for Bell Lyras

Frontier Song

Hail! Hail! The Gangs All Here

from "The Pirates of Penzance"
Solo or Duet for Bell Lyras

Sir ARTHUR SULLIVAN

The Key of E♭

81

Etude in E♭

SCHROEDER

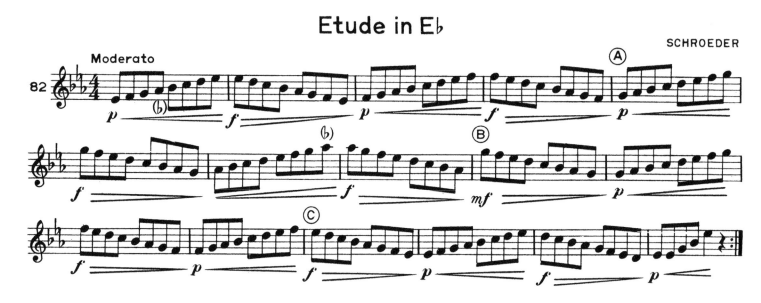

Oh! Susanna

STEPHEN C. FOSTER

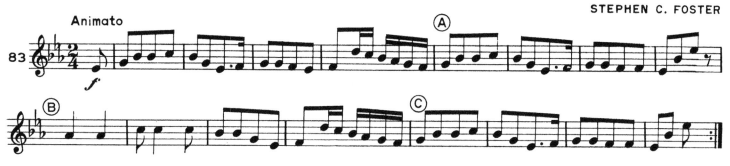

Drink to Me Only With Thine Eyes

English Air

Skaters Waltz
Solo or Duet for Bell Lyras

E. WALDTEUFEL

Old Black Joe
Solo or Duet for Bell Lyras

STEPHEN C. FOSTER

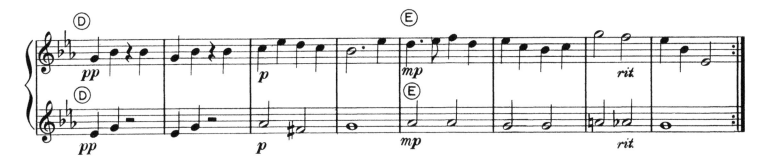

The Key of A♭

87

Etude in A♭

SCHROEDER

88

Processional March

HAYDN

89

Nightfall

FRANZ ABT

90

Excerpt from
William Tell
Solo or Duet for Bell Lyras

ROSSINI

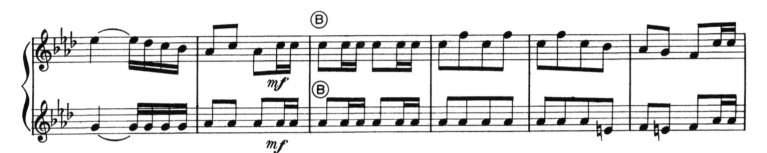

The Key of D♭

Advanced Etude in D♭

for the Development of Technical Facility

CUNIOT-HURY
Op.71, No.4

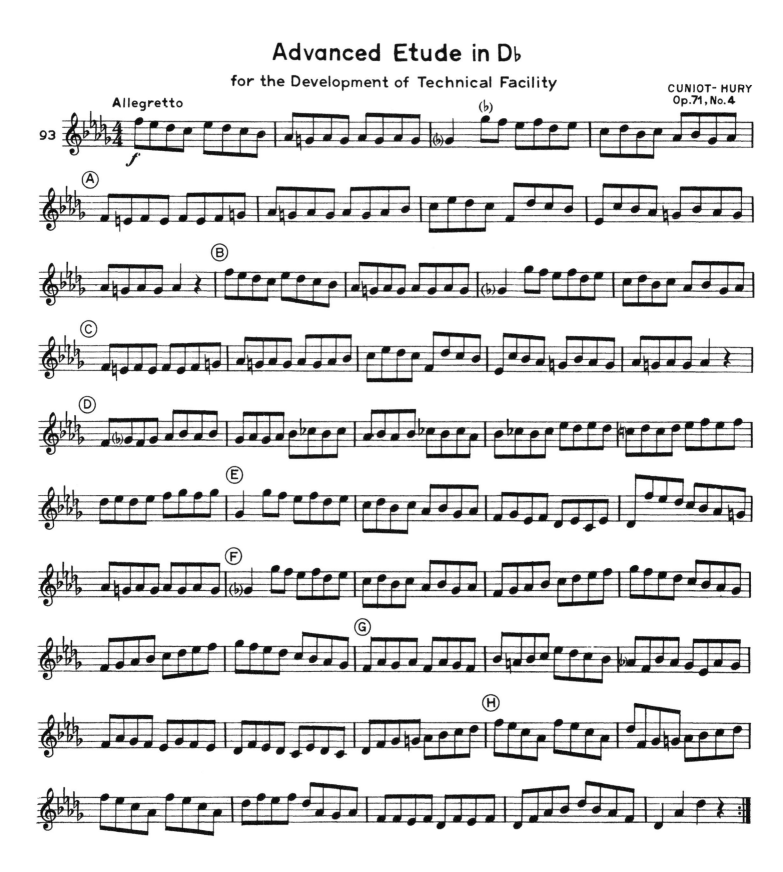

Silent Night
Solo or Duet for Bell Lyras

FRANZ GRUBER

Adeste Fidelis
Solo or Duet for Bell Lyras

JOHN READING

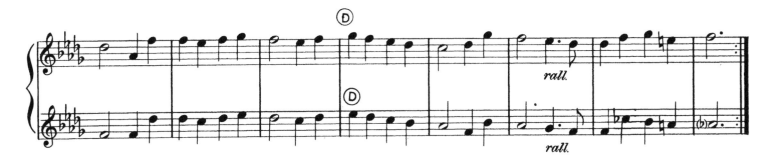

Largo

from "New World Symphony"

Bell Lyra Solo with Piano Accompaniment

Bell Lyra in C

When playing Bb Bell Lyra transpose
each note one whole step higher

DVORAK

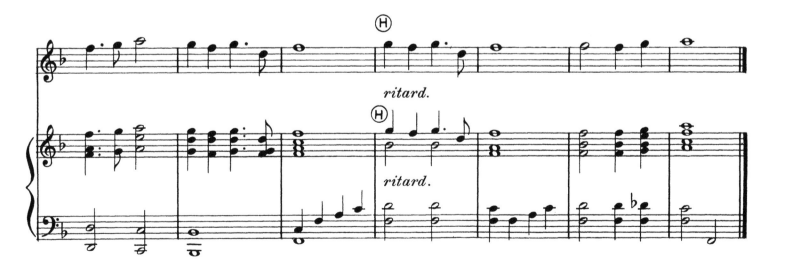

Evening Star

from "Tannhauser"

Bell Lyra Solo with Piano Accompaniment

Bell Lyra in C

> When playing B♭ Bell Lyra transpose
> each note one whole step higher

WAGNER

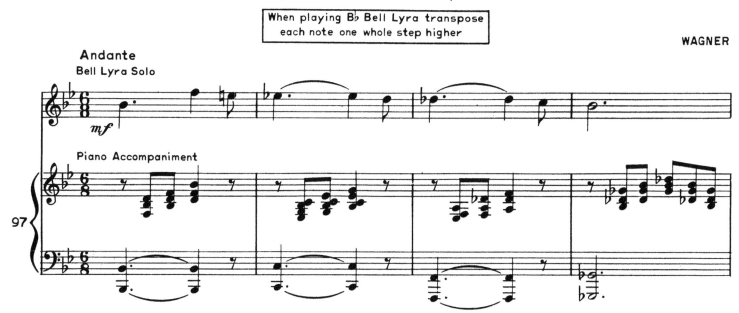

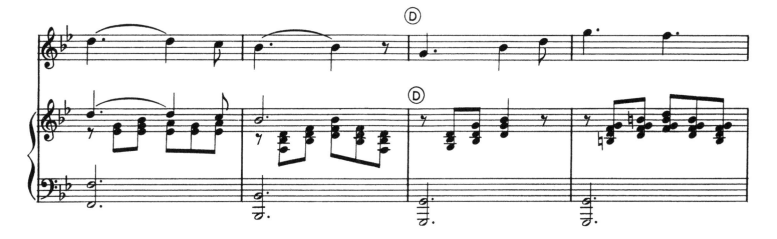

Swanee River

Bell Lyra in C

Bell Lyra Solo with Piano Accompaniment

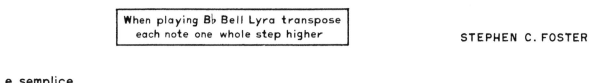

When playing B♭ Bell Lyra transpose
each note one whole step higher

STEPHEN C. FOSTER

Andante e semplice
Bell Lyra Solo

Ⓐ

Ⓑ

35

Introducing Triplets

Three notes played in the time value of two of the same kind of notes are known as a triplet. The most common type of triplets is that represented by three eighth notes. Usually a triplet is indicated by a figure 3, written above or below it.

Quarter Notes and Triplets Alternated

Pilgrims' Chorus
from "Tannhauser"

WAGNER

Andante
from "Fifth Symphony"

TSCHAIKOWSKY

Tango

ALBENIZ

The Thunderer
March

JOHN PHILIP SOUSA
Arr. by James A. Scott

Our Director
March

F. E. BIGELOW
Arr. by Harold L. Walters

High School Cadets
March

JOHN PHILIP SOUSA
Arr. by James A. Scott

Indiana State Band
March

O. R. FARRAR
Arr. by James A. Scott

March Gloria

F. H. LOSEY
Arr. by James A. Scott

Semper Fidelis

JOHN PHILIP SOUSA
Arr. by James A. Scott

BELL LYRA INTERLUDES

These novelties may effectively be used in parade routines between the musical numbers played by the full band. Featuring the Bell Lyra in such a manner adds life, color and brilliancy to the maneuvers of any marching group.

London Chimes

Repeat number as many times as desired.

The Music Box

Repeat number as many times as desired.